AIRPORT MYSTERIES

◆

The Four Business-Class Rats and
Why the Wings of Kilimanjaro Count

Deogratius Nsanzugwanko

AIRPORT MYSTERIES
THE FOUR BUSINESS-CLASS RATS AND
WHY THE WINGS OF KILIMANJARO COUNT

iUniverse books may be ordered through booksellers or by contacting:

iUniverse
1663 Liberty Drive
Bloomington, IN 47403
www.iuniverse.com
1-800-Authors (1-800-288-4677)

ISBN: 978-1-5320-6115-8 (sc)
ISBN: 978-1-5320-6116-5 (e)

Print information available on the last page.

iUniverse rev. date: 03/07/2019

Foreword

Deogratius Nsanzugwanko is a passionate novice writer who has chosen to share his memoirs chronicling the last ten years and the trips he has made abroad, within Africa and outside the continent. He shares what caused him to travel and what he was doing on his travels. He also shares the good and the bad things he has seen and forecasts what will bring change for the better of humankind both in his country, Tanzania, and the rest of the world. Chapter 1 is about his travels from Africa to Europe. In chapter 2, he talks about elections and governance. Election observations are discussed in chapter 3. In chapter 4, he gives a narrative of his travel to the UK and makes his case for the monitoring and evaluating of projects. He also discusses the emergency situation of handling elections in India and the development attained here, as well as all the strengths in fighting to achieve excellence in world competition in tourism, infrastructure development, and agriculture. Other chapters discuss violence and risk mitigation, as well as economic thoughts about how we could be manning our corporate businesses, such as trains, tourism, and mining. He insists on having a positive attitude when it comes to customer-to-business relationships (and vice versa).

Acknowledgments

This book is the product of my own memory. However, it includes the experience and wisdom of literally hundreds of colleagues, family members, friends, and others. I am unable to mention them, but they have all sparked the energy I needed to finish this book and are highly appreciated. The writing skills and choice of topics are the sole responsibility of the author, although the editors of the manuscript have played a significant role in rephrasing sentences and rearranging the content.

I also acknowledge the profound and outstanding contribution made by iUniverse in framing and editing the manuscript and for their constructive input. I also thank friends and family members for their even criticism and editing of the manuscript.

I would be selfish if I did not mention three of my writing motivators for their tireless inspirational skills.

Terri Savelle Foy, for her inspirational YouTube lectures.

Ernest Boniface Makulilo, for his Facebook Live conferences, inspiring most of his friends and acquaintances to start writing even one book.

Tanya Pergola (author of *Time Is Cows: Timeless Wisdom of the Maasai*), renowned yoga trainer and an anthropologist, for her inspiration about book writing.

Former vice president of Botswana, David N. Magang, who retired from politics and became an entrepreneur and author, for his inspirational act of going from statehouse elite to author.

Last but not least, advocate Ipilinga Panya, for chipping in with advice when the publishers asked me to amend the book title.

Deogratius Nsanzugwanko
Kisarawe, Tanzania

From Julius Nyerere International Airport to Carthage De Tunis

Between November 12, 2005, and November 20, 2005, I traveled from Dar Es Salaam (Tanzania) to Tunis (Tunisia) to attend the World Summit on Information Society, Phase II, whose theme was bridging the digital divide between the developed and least developed countries and their citizens. I received my invitation in French, which read as follows:

> Bonjour,
>
> Le Ministère des Affaires Etrangères organise une table ronde "Accès public à Internet" dans le cadre du SMSI qui se tiendra à Tunis du 14 au 19 novembre prochains (évènements parallèles inclus). L'objectif est le suivant : faciliter la rencontre entre réseaux de points d'accès public à Internet (ADEN, EPN …) et confronter les expériences par un dialogue entre praticiens. La table-ronde est prévue le 16 novembre à 16h.

A cette occasion, nous sommes heureux de vous inviter à participer à cette table ronde et, plus généralement, au SMSI.

Votre billet d'avion à destination de Tunis et votre hébergement sur place seront financés par nos soins.

Arrivée à Tunis le 13 novembre. Départ de Tunis le 20 novembre. Merci de confirmer votre disponibilité pour ces dates ou d'indiquer celles qui vous conviennent au sein de cette période. **ATTENTION: une fois vos dates précisées, elles ne pourront être changées!**

Merci de vous assurer que vous êtes enregistré auprès d'une institution de votre pays accréditée pour le Sommet ou que vous faites partie de la délégation nationale de votre pays.

Pejout

English translation:

Good day,

The French Department of Foreign Affairs is organizing a roundtable on "Public Access to the Internet" during the WSIS, Tunis, November 14–19, 2005 (parallel events included). This roundtable aims at gathering networks of public access to the internet (ADEN and others …) and confronting experiences through a debate between people involved in this field. The roundtable is scheduled for the November 16 at 4:00 p.m.

We are delighted to invite you to participate to this roundtable and, more generally, to the WSIS.

Your flight to Tunis and your stay on site will be funded by us. Arrival in Tunis on November 13. Departure from Tunis on November 20. Please confirm your availability for these dates, or advise on dates that suit you within that period. **Attention: Once you confirm your dates, they won't be changed!**

Please make sure you are registered with an institution of your country that is accredited for the summit or that you are part of the national delegation of your country.

I was filled with excitement and delighted to receive such an invitation, not only because I was going to receive professional exposure but also because I knew I would travel by air. This was my first experience in a plane, for I had never traveled outside my country. With a life limited in so many ways by a lack of resources, I could not afford this expensive means of travel. I quickly provided my response. It read as follows:

Dear sir,

I am delighted to receiving this invitation and am looking forward to receiving a formal invitation for processing of other legal documents. Can you scan the invitation letter and send it to me by email? Also I am confirming my availability on these dates to attend the roundtable discussion and definitely the WSIS.

With best regards,
Deogratius Raphael Nsanzugwanko

After several back-and-forth exchanges of documents, I submitted my passport application for the first time, and I was lucky to get it in three weeks. I encountered many ups and downs in the process of getting my passport done, with much questioning by the immigration department. Our country has since designed and launched an e-passport service that will eliminate all these calamities and the silly questioning by immigration officers. This should eliminate all the possibilities for bribes and unnecessary delays when citizens are applying for passports. The e-passport portal will be informative and easy to understand while reducing the time it takes to follow up manually before a passport can be processed. In the future, passports will be issued to any citizen wishing to have one, regardless of whether he or she is traveling abroad.

I got my passport on October 28, 2005. After that, I arranged for my international vaccination card at Mnazi-Mmoja Hospital, and I had my visa processed by the French embassy. The WSIS II organized a Tunisian visa upon landing, but I had to get my Schengen transit visa, as I had to travel through Amsterdam and Paris, as all the possible African routes were fully booked.

On the departure date, I arrived at the airport around nine o'clock at night and checked in successfully. I had to ask many questions during the check-in procedure because it was my first trip by air as an international traveler and I was alone. Thank God for my education, which allowed me to navigate this process fairly easily. I managed to get myself checked into the final boarding lounge. I wandered here and there, looking for an empty seat. Finally, I sat next to a young English lady traveling from Songea to London/ Birmingham via Amsterdam. We had a lot to talk about before we boarded the plane. I remember her telling me to buy lots of chewing gum to help relieve ear pain. She also advised me to take a lot of food and water onto the plane.

As we sat there, a few minutes before departure, that's when the real story began.

Four big rats scurried from one corner of the lounge to another. All the passengers were astonished, and many people were laughing. In the end, an old white lady made the joke "These are business-class rats." The crowd laughed and laughed. I was astonished and felt somewhat ashamed. I asked myself, *How the hell could those rats run around so brazenly without waiting for the lounge to empty?*

The story of four unusual business-class passengers might appear to be a frivolous thing to an irresponsible government or its citizens. However, the way the current terminal 2 has been renovated, everyone would agree that the government had a vision, and the shame I felt in the departure lounge was likely felt by every single Tanzanian going abroad. I don't think that those four passengers had just that day to run; it was their territory, and I bet they had a schedule of a daily marathon or half of it. Shame, huh?

After that, a smooth voice on the intercom instructed all of us departing the world over by the Dutch carrier to board. The voice said, "Attention, please. All passengers traveling to Amsterdam by KLM are kindly asked to proceed through gate number five for final checkups and boarding."

I was sitting near the boarding gate, so I was among the first passengers to board. I was shown where to sit by our beautiful air hostesses. After I got myself seated, I started familiarizing myself with the magazine in front of me. After all the passengers had boarded, I heard my first-ever in-plane announcement. It was in Dutch at first, so I could not understand what was being said. However, the announcer repeated the announcement in French, and I was able to pick up a few of the little words. When the English announcement followed, I recorded it as follows (although I may have missed a few words).

"Ladies and gentlemen, welcome on board MD-11 Boeing 777, flight number [xxx], flying from Dar Es Salaam International Airport to Schiphol, Amsterdam, International Airport. We will serve you food and drinks twice during the flight. Our estimated flight time to Amsterdam is eight hours."

At that time, I couldn't differentiate planes or flights by their model; I remember that it was a fancy plane that I flew for the first time and it was doing quite well. Flying from Dar Es Salaam to

Amsterdam for eight hours only, that was a super normal speed and, I think, even with the invention of the latest plane technology, such as the Dreamliners. Having an MD-11 one was to be well equipped economically and strategically. For an airline to remain competitive, it has the strategic need to maintain different planes of different sizes, capacities, and technologies so it can cater to different market sizes. This ensures the airline will have a healthy share of the world aviation market.

After the announcement, they served us some very white papers, which confused me at first. I put them in my mouth, biting down, thinking it was crisps. Alas, the paper was soft. I saw some of my fellow passengers wiping their hands and faces, and I quickly did the same, rubbing my face gently, then my hands, then throwing the paper in the bin as the air hostess immediately came by to collect them.

We flew to Amsterdam and landed safely, but from my window, I could see the very well-developed infrastructure of flyovers, road networks, and the elegant Schiphol International Airport. I was amazed, and had some mixed bad feelings thinking of the foolish rats who could not wait until we departed to engage in their rat race. I thought of our international failure in the marathon and the Olympic Games. Maybe if we could find those rats, they could represent us, bring us gold medals and restore our national pride.

I was astonished by the beauty of the Amsterdam airport. Inside the building, it was dazzling, with signs clearly marking who should go where and where to line up for immigration clearance. It was all so properly arranged. My boarding pass was quickly stamped and I was told where I should proceed. I proceeded to gate number 23 and sat there waiting for my plane to Paris to board. Due to bad weather that day, we had a four-hour delay at the airport. Finally, we were cleared to board. Despite all the electronic moving walkways, I was astonished when an old Nigerian woman came straight up to me and lamented, "My son! Help me. Ooh. These people are not giving me clear directions, and now my plane has left."

"Where are you going?" I asked.

"Cologne, and my flight is at 11:00 a.m. Oh, please help me."

"Where is your boarding pass?" I asked.

She showed me her boarding pass, and I walked downstairs with her and found her boarding gate. It was easy. After getting her seated and telling her to wait for her plane, which would arrive in sixty minutes, she told me, "Wait, my son. Take this magazine and read it, and God will bless you."

It was a Jehovah's Witness magazine, and I did feel as if I was blessed as I turned back to head to my boarding gate. As I write this book, I still remember that lady, and I feel she owes me a visit so we can catch up and share the lighthearted embarrassing moment she had at Schiphol. On the other hand, that moment to me was so enriching, exposing me not only to the airport gates but to how people of other countries resemble each other. Every time I say my prayers, I think of the lady I met who gave me a Jehovah's Witness magazine after I refused her monetary gift. What a blessing. When she asked me how much she should pay me for my service, I thought of our culture and our education system: Can you really charge someone simply for showing him or her the proper route to take? Can you charge someone for such a small help? In our schools, we were taught to respect elders and we were raised in communal societies. Did they not do the same in Nigerian life? I asked myself so many questions, and I have not been able to figure out why that old lady asked me how much she needed to pay me.

The way Schiphol International Airport was built reminds me of how poorly the JNIA terminal 2 was constructed and deteriorated at that time. Maybe we will reach those standards in our newly constructed terminal 3 at the JNIA; and I will once again praise the good work of our government. I imagine that in fifty years, our sons, daughters, and grandchildren will enjoy the good life. Let's all urge the government to continue striving for all the best aspects of life. Just try to imagine how the situation was in most government hospitals in 2005. How about public schools? Roads? Access to water and education? How was electrical conductivity in our townships and villages? How many megawatts in total were there? How many bitumen standard roads where there? What is the situation like at the moment? Have the hospitals improved? The roads? Not to mention our airports and the new terminal 3 at Julius Nyerere International Airport.

The Standard Gauge Railway Project also says a lot about our country. Our railway network almost collapsed, and operations within that system were manned awkwardly at best. Bookings, information sharing, and locomotive management are all in need of improvement. Will business information systems reengineering take place in all these projects? Will the authorities train their operations managers to work professionally, and will customer relations systems improve? Assuming these projects are completed, how can we assure the timing will be right to maximize their potential? When the regime changes, the standard gauge railway and all other projects will likely collapse.

How about our schools? Have secondary schools in each ward improved? Do we have tangible proof of the acclaimed successes of all the projects? Have we made available to people information on changes in public policy and public policy management? I urge the authorities to monitor the results that were promised in all these projects and policy-implementation programs. Who are the people manning these projects? Will these people look like those educational managers of the Kondoa District, who leaked a standard VII final examination to the kids so they could all pass? Will it mirror the mismanagement of our government projects, poor exposure to innovations and business transformation? Is all this the result of people who passed their schooling because they got help from their parents and teachers, leaking the standard VII, form IV, and form VI examination papers?

Shame on us all. Let us strive to build a society of responsible citizens, citizens who love their country with their whole hearts, citizens who strive for fulfillment in all aspects of their daily lives.

With the completion of terminal 3, I'm betting terminal 2 will be serving local flights. Our ATCL used to lease only one flight. Without the recent purchases of six brand new flights, all these construction projects would have been useless. We might have extra buildings, but we will receive nothing in terms of air service, as foreign investors will be shut out. However, if ATCL lowers its prices and increases its local routes, they can simultaneously make a profit while helping build a society of civilized people. If ATCL operates in all national parks, accommodating tourists to the Serengeti, Manyara, the Loliondo Game Controlled Area, Katavi National Park, Gombe and Mahale National Parks, Ruaha National Park, Selous National Park, Moyowosi, Burigi, and Rwakimisi Game Controlled Areas, and so many more tourist attractions, profits will boom and hence boost our national economy. The investment in building is tremendous, and I would, on my own behalf, call upon all Tanzanians to embrace these investments and do what is expected from them and contribute with a remarkable share of our nation's GDP.

We left Amsterdam at one in the afternoon and flew to Paris. It took us only forty-five minutes to touch base. The pilot made an announcement.

"Good afternoon, ladies and gentlemen. We sincerely apologize once again for the delay at Schiphol in Amsterdam. The delay was due to bad weather at Charles de Gaulle International Airport. They could not receive any more flights due to the weather …"

We arrived in Paris, and we had to wait four or five hours at Charles de Gaulle International Airport before we could board Air France to Carthage International Airport in Tunis, Tunisia. Charles de Gaulle is not only as developed as all other major international airports, but the management of passengers in all aspects, such as immigration, airport transfers, etc., is more advanced and civilized.

The connection of all other means of transport, such as bus stops and railway stations, takes place within structures that would have been imitated by our newly constructed terminal 3 and standard gauge railway stations of Dar Es Salaam, Morogoro, Dodoma, Tabora, Kigoma, Shinyanga, and Mwanza and other big stops like Chalinze, Kilosa, Saranda, Manyoni, Itigi, Tura, Urambo, Bukene, Isaka, Malampaka, Kailua, Nguruka, and Uvinza.

How is our standard gauge railway route structured? Will it make sure it improves between airports and railway transfers? Are we planning the standard gauge railway for inter-region connectivity? Do we have a master plan for railway connectivity between all major cities for, say, the next one hundred years? In a hundred years, will we need to improve those structures again? I urge authorities to make some major changes in the cities of Morogoro, Dodoma, Tabora, Kigoma, and Mwanza, to allow all-in-one stations for air, railway, and bus transfers. Moreover, the Dar Es Salaam Central Stations should be planned at Pugu Railway Station so they can link city suburb railways, such as Pugu Mloganzila–Kibaha–Bagamoyo; Pugu–Dar Ubungo–Mbezi–Bunju–Bagamoyo, and Pugu–Chanika–Mvuti–Chamazi Mbagala–Kigamboni.

Our flight from Paris to Tunis Carthage Airport took two and a half hours. We were all conveyed in buses and dropped off at the registration center, where we were all registered, weighed, and tested for blood pressure, height, and weight. Finally, we were given IDs for the conferences at Kram PalExpo before we were taken to our respective hotels. At the Hotel De Touring Club, it was a very cool environment, facing the Mediterranean Ocean.

Not many fishermen were seen on the ocean at night. Maybe it wasn't a fishing season. However, the fish dishes on the hotel menu were just amazing.

At the airport, during both our arrival and departure, I was amazed by the number of airplanes with the Air Tunis charter. I counted more than thirty planes and asked myself, *Is this an African state?* Definitely yes, so why is it that we have only one ATR Dash

800, and it's not even ours? We are just leasing it, and I hear that we are not even making money and that the number of employees of this broke, collapsing corporation is overwhelming. What is our real problem? Our national career really counts, and kudos to you, Mr. President, for I believe this will be a good start. In the near future, we may see our giraffe in the international skies again, as most of the Tenth Parliament's MPs have been lamenting.

Hongera mzee chapa kazi ujenge urithi wa vizazi vijavyo (congratulations, sir, keep up the good work for the future of our generations to come).

The following six days were intense, with discussions, conferences, presentations, and showcases of the various information and communications technologies conducted worldwide. I attended several of them, and they provided a real eye-opener in the field of information technology. One interesting project was that of a colleague. We were staying at the same hotel, and he was from Canada.

"Our projects have targeted people who are living in distant places, and most of the time, their areas are covered by heavy snow. So what we do is have them go online and describe their medical conditions, and our consulting doctors prescribe medications for them, which we deliver using drones."

Another interesting showcase was done at the Tanzania Pavilion, in which the characters demonstrated the digital transformation using the analogy of analog phones to mobile phones, using faxes during ancient times, and instantly sending images in these mobile times. If you could've been there, I believe you would have laughed on that day as we did.

I also had fun, having dinners full of lamb dishes and so many other delicious foods with friends and colleagues. I would urge the government to initiate commercialized animal farming, including goats, cows, and other livestock to establish both internal and outside markets as a source of income to boost our mineral-based economy sectors. Animal husbandry, fishing ponds, lakes, and oceans need to be commercialized. We should leave alone the transportation sector because, I imagine, what would the SGR and the ATCL's Bombardiers, Dreamliners, or airbus do if we didn't have enough resources to transfer from regions to main cities? Where will our people get all the money to spend on air and land transports if they are not capacitated?

I remember a friend I met at the conference mentioning reading her emails at home. I asked, "Are you connected to the internet at home?" She was surprised by my question. What the hell was I talking about? But for me, this was a real-life case of the digital divide in Tanzania. How many homes were connected to the internet in 2005? Were the prices of hardware and software affordable? Was it user friendly? I highly commend the move taken by the International Telecommunications Unit and the UN Trade Organization for their efforts. We have seen vast developments in the information and communication technologies sector, and in my opinion, the digital divide has been somewhat bridged. However, per capita expenditures for connectivity remain extremely high for the least-developed countries. I would urge the organizations and individuals responsible for this to come up with a way to negotiate these prices and hence attain a quality digital connection and a high-quality digital life.

On my way back from Tunis, it was a day trip, and hence I enjoyed watching the snow on the mountain peaks of the Alps, which span France, Italy, Switzerland, Austria, Slovenia, Liechtenstein, Germany, and possibly Hungary. I was reminded of our African border issues in countries like Tanzania and the DRC, Burundi, Rwanda, Uganda, Kenya, Mozambique, Malawi, and Zambia, thinking about how volatile some parts are and how our nations have successfully managed to live peacefully for decades. I'm not saying there are no issues, but the fact that all the countries mentioned live in peace and harmony is something we need to take pride in.

After landing in France, then Amsterdam, we boarded a Kenya Airways flight flying between Amsterdam and Nairobi. We had delicious meals, and the flight itself was comfortable and fancy. I continued wondering, why the hell are Kenyans making it to Europe while we cannot afford internal flights?

On my arrival in Tanzania, I shared a light moment with friends and colleagues, and I came to realize that ATCL was the first to be approached by KLM Royal Dutch Airlines for a partnership. They refused. This reminded me of my MBA class about mergers and acquisitions, where you need to be very strong or have well-trained business analysts to help you chart the entire course of action, including marketing, product design, product life cycles, and consumers and/or consumer psychology.

By knowing what phase of the aviation business lifecycle we are in, we could have identified the general corporate strategy to help us enter into the market vehemently and compete. We can now also identify the prevailing customer groups, as defined by the consumer adoption curve. There are five distinct customer groups, each characterized by a set of beliefs, motivations, and behaviors:

- **Innovators.** Innovators are the first to adopt a new product. They are willing to take risks, are youngest in age, have the highest social class, have great financial liquidity, are very social, and have the closest contact to influential sources and interaction with other innovators. Mr. President, I clearly identify you as one of the innovators in today's democracy. Nevertheless, although you are willing and able to innovate our macro-economies, strategies, and policies, don't forget to forge synergies with the finest brains of our country, never forgetting to ensure those who are manning our projects have a changed mind-set and etiquette, in general, to ensure excellence is attained at all levels.

- **Early adopters.** This is the second fastest category of individuals who adopt an innovation. Early adopters have the highest degree of opinion leadership among the other adopter categories. They are typically younger in age, have higher social status, have more financial lucidity and advanced education, and are more socially forward than late adopters. I would plead to all your government principals and seniors to strive for this behavior, for they are the ones implementing your programs, policy influencers, and overseers on your behalf. Are you real satisfied with them all? Or do you just get along with some of them whose behavior does not satisfy you? Do you have a well assessment report of their behaviors? If yes, where would you place them in the DISC curve? How is their interaction and professional cooperation so they can ensure maximum or effective productivity? That's your own task and enjoy the leading or the hiring and firing.

- **Early majority.** Individuals in this category adopt our product after a varying degree of time. This time of adoption is significantly longer than for the innovators and early adopters. Early majority people tend to be slower in the adoption process, have above-average social status, have contact with early adopters, and seldom hold positions of opinion leadership or influence. All government senior staff and employees who hold diplomas and degrees at different levels will have to switch their behavior in such a direction. Now linking with your newly reformed ATCL limited how high have they taken time to promoting and pricing their products while observing these differences? How about promotional prices for university students? Or the sick referred to major referral hospitals?

- **Late majority.** Late-majority folks will adopt an innovation after the average member of society. They approach a new product with a high degree of skepticism and only after the majority of society has already adopted the product. They are also typically skeptical about an innovation, have below-average social status, have very little financial lucidity, are in contact with others in the late majority and early majority, and have very little opinion leadership. Our countrymen at large will have to imitate your positive and strong instincts and directives so as to live in a well-mannered and managed life.

- **Laggards.** These guys are the last to adopt. These individuals typically have an aversion to change and tend to be advanced in age. Laggards tend to be focused on "traditions," and they are likely to have the lowest social status, have the lowest financial fluidity, be oldest of all other adopters, and be in contact with only family and close friends. Tanzanians at large, let's change our attitudes, whatever our social class might be. Let's learn to be innovators, as our lovely president is, and/or early adopters to help move forward our country's development agenda.

So where are we as consumers? We are consuming flights and other services and products as well, but do we really know why we are consuming them? Can we really justify our consuming routes and budget and the lives we're left with after consuming as a nation? Do we have the right people with the capacity to advise on our consuming strategy? Do we have a consuming vision? Stand still, think, and find the answers for yourself and your family, or for yourself and your people, and in the end, just evaluate the multiplier effect of the consuming we are doing and the cost associated with our consumption. Is it advantageous, or are we making losses? If Kenyans could get their shit together by having planes as big as the one I saw before 2005, then we should all commend a job well done by Mr. President Magufuli in reviving ATCL by purchasing the first three Bombardiers, two Airbuses, and a Dreamliner in our skies to date. Again for the recent Airbus and Dreamliner order our country has made It is my hope that, come 2020–2025, he will leave this country with a fully fledged air company that will compete not only locally but internationally.

Do you see any rats running in your vision? In your business area, studies, home, or workplace? Do you remember the four business-class rats I mentioned earlier? Are you aware of your work environment or business area's vision and structure? What is this vision we are talking about? As we continue our discussion let's have a hint on the power of vision, in trying to answer the question, "What is vision?"

Vision is like the eye of the eagle. An eagle sees farther than any other animal. In the same way, vision allows you to look into the future and see a life filled with meaning and purpose. Mr. President Magufuli, you are an eagle. So if you are an eagle, who is our vice president? How about our prime minister? And the other ministers? Permanent secretaries? Or directors and board chairmen? It could be wise if they could all be baby eagles to echo your powerful vision and generosity.

Vision is like a magnifying glass. A magnifying glass brings objects into clearer focus. Vision for your country and or workplace or even your homes and families, allows you to see your life with better clarity.

Vision is like the banks of a river. The banks of the river provide direction for the flow of the water. Vision provides direction and keeps you moving in the way you want to go. But I worry who the hell would be the next president after your first term or the second if you win the coming general election in the year 2020? I would urge your government to try develop systems which will hinder deterioration of the good works you have accomplished and those that you will accomplish plus the good ones accomplished by your predecessors or else our country at large would be unrestrained, which means without a vision for the future. And that would mean you would not have a clear purpose in life.

Will it attract rats, or will it visualize a right business idea for a lucrative profit-making business, with well-defined structures? Do you see profit booming and advancement in the provision of social services? Be the people you want to see. Be the countrymen you are imagining. Be the society you want for your children, grandchildren, and great-grandchildren. Be responsible: remove all the rats in your planning, execution, and evaluation.

No rats!

OR Tambo International Airport

I travelled from Dar Es Salaam in May 2007 to Johannesburg, South Africa. On my route, I was reminded of South Africa's political struggles toward independence and the partnership that was forged by the Tanzanian government and the black African National Congress government. When boarding the South African Airways plane, so many questions arose within my inner self. For a country suffering through apartheid and the locking up of the famous Nelson Mandela, how could they possibly have a big, neat, clean airplane like this? What would their airport look like? Would I see rats or a deteriorating infrastructure? Upon landing at OR Tambo, I was astonished by the beauty of the airport. It was a serious operation, with well-mannered business processes. In South Africa, all the good things—economy, good jobs, land, education—were white-dominated. However, the road network linking the South African cities was not. The country was well built and well planned, and it seems they have a plan for the future. Do our national authorities strive for the same standard? Is Magufuli's government sensitive about seeking a better tomorrow? In my opinion, yes, the country is moving faster, and most of our country's programs have been clearly put in place. Our government is improving in every sector, and I pray that in twenty years, most of our cities will be well built.

However, I would urge our governments to establish a clear plan for our cities for, say, the next fifty years. This will include land for industries, playgrounds, substations, fire departments, markets, automobile markets, fruit bazaars, and farmland, clearly marked and supported by infrastructure to allow for major investment in agriculture and other areas. If we don't plan for proper land use, even our industrialization vision will be rendered somewhat meaningless. The country can even build some industrial buildings and encourage local investors to invest in predefined sectors.

However, in countries like Tanzania, where we blacks have dominated in every sector since independence, why the hell is our economy one of the poorest, and why has our government been lamented for carelessness, embezzlement of government funds, poor education institutions, poor infrastructure, and so forth? What is the main problem underpinning our development and provision of good social services? That being said, the government of the day is doing everything possible to rescue the situation. Try to imagine removing the residents along the Kipawa and Karakata areas, with the aim of improving the JNIA infrastructure. Bear in mind that I do not minimize the development efforts taken by the past four governments; neither did I say the government of the day doesn't. However, if the management of ATCL continues operating as they used to, I believe we will go nowhere. From Bombardier to Boeing 787 Dreamliners, managers are needed who can truly turn around organizations and business processes, as Oman Air did. Kindly, Mr. President, establish clear, targeted results and hire managers who will come not only to raise ATCL to great heights but also to improve the entire sector of air travel in Tanzania. We need people who offer results, not just talk. Find a guru, someone who seriously considers your vision of revamping our "giraffe in the skies."

Who are the people manning the departments and sections within ATCL? Do they have the qualities required? I was once astonished to hear a pilot termed as a "director of operations." Really? Have I underestimated his qualities and qualifications?

Kindly let me know of his education and other qualifications. In my opinion, this pilot would have made chief pilot or higher. If he was so competent, why not make him head of a section in the technical department so he can be used as a helper to the director of operations and business development?

South African cities are constructed effectively; likewise, I would urge Tanzania's government authorities to come up with each city's master plan, which will help them determine land use for the next one hundred years.

At the training session, I met brothers and sisters from most of the African states, including Malawi, Mozambique, South Africa, Botswana, Lesotho, Swaziland, Democratic Republic of Congo, and Zambia. Apart from the "Train the Facilitator" course, we had fun, and I enjoyed the spirit of African brotherhood. A colleague from Mozambique was boasting of his family's coffee farms and explaining how rich his family had become due to farming. Despite his bragging, he was kind enough to share a drink, a mojito, and he had a sense that some areas of Dar Es Salaam were just as well structured as the areas of Pretoria and Johannesburg, only we needed to improve our public infrastructure, sewage systems, and the like. Our chat reminded me of the war, where our African soldiers died and how we made many blood sacrifices in liberating Mozambique by helping FRELIMO, who was battling with RENAMO, the right-wing guerrillas. Thousands of people died before they finally got their independence in 1975. I remembered Samora Moses Marcel and how he died. There is much to discuss about our front-line leaders, who dared to risk their lives in search for equality and human dignity in Africa. These include Kwame Nkurumah, Patrice Emely Lumumba, Julius Nyerere, Chris Hann, Walter Sisulu, Johachim Chisano, Joshua Nkomo, Robert Gabriel Mugabe, and so many more. Mozambique is a unique African destination, offering beautiful beaches, wild game reserves, diving escapes, swimming with dolphins, and so much more. Mozambique also has kind local people, fresh markets, rich historical sites, and a rich history including slavery, spice trading, and exports of homegrown nuts and cotton. Can our Bombardier plan a route to Mozambique? Is it going to be a visa-free route, like the South African route? Can all African states remove visa requirements for Africa's brothers and sisters who want to go to the beaches or to all the national parks and game reserves across the continent? How about all the water parks and wildlife safaris? Mozambique is rich, but how is the economy? How are the mighty Limpopo and Zambezi rivers utilized economically? Yet, how are we utilizing our rivers? The Malagarasi River on the west? How about the Rufiji River? Kudos to the government of Tanzania for starting the construction of the hydropower project on the Rufiji River on the Selous game reserve. The power output will increase by almost two thousand megawatts, which will add to the national grid and hence contribute to the country's industrialization efforts. How are the heavy rains being utilized to maximize the country's GDP? Will they merely end up being a source of poverty and displacement due to heavy floods? How about its balance of payments? Will the exports in aluminum, cashew nuts, cotton, and sugar supersede imports? And how about Tanzania's balance of payments? Reform, reform, and reform. Yes, reform our land use plan, reform all the title deeds releasing procedures, reform all the surveyed areas roads and routes, reform the system of government sales tax and revenue collections. Reform or else you will be reformed in the end where you shall see many of your people in court as a result of embezzlements, frauds, and the like.

After contemplating these issues relating to Mozambique and Tanzania, let me highlight our training. It was composed of modules such as access to polling stations, registration of voters, media and elections, campaign financing, civil society, voter education, registration technologies, procurement and logistics, distribution of elections material and equipments, voter roll problems, electoral management bodies' independence, electoral phases (preelectoral, electoral period phase, and postelectoral phases) and management of the entire electoral process (nominations of candidates, electoral campaign, voting, results declaration, tallying, and verification). We spoke about African politics, civilization, and global trends in politics, and it made me think of our situation in Africa. I thought of the history of Johnas Savimbi in Angola, Joseph Konyi in Uganda, the Rwandan genocide, Burundian refugees, Boko Haram, Interahamwe, M23, the Kibiti rebels, and Alshabaab, just to mention a few. Is this the Africa we want? Let us commend all the efforts made by African governments to curb terrorism and maintain peace and tranquility in our nations.

As a reminder, or as an introduction for those who don't have a background in elections or politics, I am going to share with you a formula for an election cycle. It is based on a training digest we had in Pretoria, and I believe that if all the key players and stakeholders are obliged to play a role, we may achieve free, fair, and democratic elections. There are many phases to the electoral process: these include the design and drafting of legislation, the recruitment and training of electoral staff, electoral planning, voter registration, the registration of political parties, nomination of parties and candidates, the electoral campaign, polling, counting, the tabulation of results, the declaration of results, the resolution of electoral disputes, reporting, auditing, and archiving. After the end of one electoral process, it is desirable that work on the next begins: the whole process can be described as the "electoral cycle." After thinking clearly about the training and what it constituted, I have decided to develop the following formula to summarize what one might wish to learn as an electoral official. The formula is totally my invention, and it depicts my thinking. Scholars are welcome to develop and further this thinking.

Election management is considered both a scientific activity and an art. It is a science because of several reasons: it has universally accepted principles, it has a cause-and-effect relationship, it can be calculated, it can be extrapolated, it can be forecasted and all players can project at every election district how the results are going to be, it can be manipulated, and it can be played with. If a political party enters into an election disregarding numbers, or without a clear analysis of winning and losing then they better stay calm or never waste resources or be ready to surprised by the electoral results where they will rejoice if they win or grieve if they lose. At the same time, it is an art because it requires perfection through practice, practical knowledge, creativity, personal skills, etc. So, for free, fair, and credible elections, the electoral management bodies and the officers charged with coordinating the conduct of elections need to be independent and unbiased. The process itself needs extra care and must be well managed.

In my quantitative techniques and decision theories, we were taught that $Y = f(x)$.

Now, if $Y = f(x)$,

Therefore, $Y = {}_\alpha\int^\alpha \sum(x_{1+X2 + X3+ Sn +Dn})$

Where Y = free, fair, independent, and credible elections delivered to a country.

X_1, X_2, X_3 = preelectoral phase, electoral phase, and postelectoral phase in the election cycle, respectively.

S_n = spices, which stands for all legal traits that contribute to free, fair, and independent elections. These things include but are not limited to participatory and inclusive electoral processes, well-trained media, the four pillars of democracy (stakeholders, civil service organizations, and observers), missions, political party aspirants, curious learners, faith-based organization, and the like, which are experienced at manning the electoral process. Mind you, an election can be held without these traits, but for an election to meet international standards, it must meet the qualities of the S_n category, and it needs to be very well managed to deliver a credible, free, and fair election.

D_n = drama.

For an election to be successfully delivered, the electoral management bodies must also clearly and effectively manage the drama of candidates, politicians, political parties, and civil service organizations. The drama and spice levels would be different, or less stressful, at each phase of the electoral process, as earlier defined.

α = the end result after the entire process is integrated and the output summed up. This might be termed as a successful or unsuccessful delivery of an election. In short, it is the end result after the election, being either a peaceful state or a state of violence and war and the like.

I kept on thinking of how refugees were flocking in numbers into the United Republic of Tanzania from our neighboring countries of Rwanda, Burundi, and the Democratic Republic of Congo, and I realized that if the equation above was clearly managed by responsible institutions, with transparent processes and mechanisms, including all key stakeholders who are prepared to accept what whatever outcome, then the problems of civil war and the like would be unlikely.

Take the Democratic Republic of Congo, the largest country in Africa, for example. It is rich in terms of minerals and other natural resources—and our country played a role in eliminating the rebellion group M23 That group operated in the province of North Kivu and Eastern Congo. Who created the group? What was their primary purpose? And in whose interest was it formed? But kudos to the recent elections where the nightmare was played out. Imagine the burning of electoral warehouse few days before elections? This made CENI postpone elections for seven days and they really delivered. Here they are with a newly elected president not disregarding the complaints of other contestants who were legally refuted after they filed a case.

3

Good Evening, Khomasdaal

In the evening of November 19, 2009, I touched down at Hosea Kutako International Airport as an election observer in Namibia's general elections under the Electoral Forum of the Southern Africa Development Cooperation. I wondered why we were landing in an empty airport with no buildings other than the terminal. I expected to see or hear that the airport was called Sam Nujoma International Airport, after the first SWAPO president of Namibia. Why the hell was it Hosea Kutako? Who was this, and what was it all about?

I came to learn that this airport is the hub for Air Namibia, and it was named Hosea Kutako after Chief Hosea Komombumbi Kutako (born 1870 at Okahurimehi, near Kalkfeld, died July 18, 1970, in the Aminuis Reserve). Kutako was an early Namibian nationalist leader and a founding member of Namibia's first nationalist party, the SWANU. Hosea Kutako, alongside the British Anglican priest Rev. Michael Scott, submitted numerous petitions to the United Nations during the 1950s and 1960s, calling on the world body to end South African rule and grant Namibia independence. This eventually led to the UN's recognition of Namibia as a sovereign country under colonial administration by South Africa. The historic 1971 advisory opinion of the International Court of Justice was that South Africa's continued administration of Namibia was illegal under the terms of international law. Hosea Kutako is considered a national hero in Namibia.

This airport is about forty-five kilometers outside Windhoek, or, as it is popularly known, Khomasdaal. At that time, the population was two million people. However, Air Namibia is doing quite well, with a fleet large enough to bring home profits and an advanced lifestyle. I remember seeing a Germany flight disembarking hundreds of tourists and businessmen. There is a lot of tourism in that southwestern country, ranging from the Kalahal to the Walvis Bay beach hotels.

Epangelo Mining is a mining company owned by the government. It was founded in 2009 with the aim of governing the rights on six mineral resources deemed strategic for Namibia and for which new exploration rights must be held by the government. The six resources are diamonds, gold, coal, uranium, copper, and rare-earth minerals. Tanzania has a lot to learn from these mineral-manning strategies. Who is manning our diamonds at Mwadui? What do we get from the western gold ridge of Kahama, Kakola, Geita, Biharamulo, Kibondo, and Nyamongo? Does the data clearly show what miners take home and what we as a country get? Is it fair? If there is no fairness, we need a very strong country-wide debate on what should be done to maximize our earnings as a country while those businessmen and women investing in mines are assured of their profits in their business ventures. Do you remember the meeting of the miners association of Tanzania members and the president on 22nd January 2019? What did you learn from it? Is there any effective system for protecting gold and other mines from being smuggled? If car tires can be used to smuggle gold, what can be done to ensure no smuggling? Do you think we need to empower our local government leaders and local government institutions at lower levels? Yes, I would urge us to change our local government acts so as to ensure that the lower levels of our local governments are useful, meaningful, and have a greater stake in the protection and sustainability of our natural resources while contributing much to our GDP at large.

Based on the facts above, extracted from Wikipedia, I would urge the government of Tanzania to forge ties with brotherly countries. When deployed to Hardap Mariental and the nearby settlements of Gibeon, Hardap, and Omaheke, I met an old man who, after we introduced ourselves as election observers, inquired about our nationalities. Our group included Professor George from the Zimbabwe Electoral Commission, a lady from the Zambia Electoral Commission, and me, from Tanzania's Electoral Commission. Immediately he grabbed my hand and asked me, "Who is that president of yours?"

Ali Hassan Mwinyi replied, "No."

Benjamin Mkapa replied, "Mhm."

Jakaya Kikwete said, "No."

Mwl Julius Nyerere hugged me, saying, "That one was a true son of Africa. How is he?"

I told him he'd been dead since 1999. He felt so sorry, and he was quite happy. We left the area and visited other places for fun after work, such as the Hardap Dam. On summing up at the Safari Court Hotel, one of the professors from the University of Namibia asked, "Are there any people from Tanzania?"

We sighed. "Yes."

He cheered, saying, "Your first president, Mwl Julius Nyerere, was a true son of Africa."

Now, if all these people recognize the contribution made by our forefathers, what advantage can we take from this? Can we fly our Bombardiers to Zimbabwe, Angola, and Namibia? Or to Botswana and South Africa? Can we leave Zambia and the RDC alone? Can we take our fisheries experts to be trained in the deep-sea fishing camps in Walvis Bay or our mining officers to be trained in mining-sector management? For a country that became independent only in 1990, but with big fleets and a well-structured economy, they offer much we can learn from. Remember I am not minimizing our development;

rather, I want us to stay alert in all aspects of management and governance so we can maximize our economic potential as a result of the good friendships we have created all along the SADC region. Is it not a shame for us to struggle while we invest in our African brothers and sisters down there? Let's get our act together and create something for the mutual benefit of our country and those of our African brothers. I know our president has shown us a way by establishing free education, increasing the budget for drugs and medication accessibility by 90 percent, and tightening government expenditure. But why are you tightening budget expenditure? It will be meaningless if this tightness never brings us tangible results and leaves us a legacy of debt for generations to come. Mr. President, enshrine our free education policy into law so that none can alter it after your time has elapsed or after you have lost the election. All the good things should go hand in hand to changing our legal framework and creating the best future for our kids and grandchildren.

We should approach tourism professionally, strategically, and competitively. I bet foreigners are benefiting from tourism more than we are. All the lodges and fancy hotels in the Serengeti and Ngorongoro Crater are charging thousands of dollars a day, but what are we earning a day? Can ATCL buy small helicopters and small planes to man the tourism sector along the Western and Northern Corridors, or South and Northwestern Tanzania? Can we build roadside tourist camps to accommodate local tourists at a low government rate? Are we expecting to increase internal tourism while leaving the accessibility conditions the same? If you depart from Arusha to Loliondo, there is no government hostel en route to support local tourism. From Loliondo to Serengeti, there is no hostel by the roadside for about two hundred kilometers in the jungle. We need to change, and I believe we must change to attract more local tourists and tourism in general.

"If we cannot reduce the cost of tourism sites, we can forget about increasing the number of local tourists. The roads must be improved for our people to move through easily while paying entrance fees and other associated costs. Say, for example, we get five million local tourists driving through our parks. This would account for almost 65 billion TZS per annum. I know you know what I want to say. If our roads are smooth throughout all the parks and our people drive through while paying gate fees only, we lose out on the multiplier effect of their visits as they spend money on water, drinks and food, petrol, and lubricants. I am appealing to you, Mr. President, and our nation's authorities: Overhaul our tourism sector and tourism business as you did ATCL, leasing airplanes, including ATRs, and buying three Bombardiers. Now our first-ever Dreamliner Boeing 787 and the two Airbuses have arrived in Tanzania after your being in office only two years. Kudos to you, John Joseph Pombe Magufuli.

ATCL's new Boeing 787 Dreamliner and is expected to launch on the Dar–Mumbai–Dar direct route.

In all the polling stations we visited, did you mean "voters turned out in large numbers to vote for the candidates of their preference. However, was this because all their polling stations were well arranged with water and electricity facilities? Or was it because Namibia's Electoral Commission has arranged polling to cater to all groups to the extent that they have mobile polling stations? Or is this turnout because the electorate is aware enough of what they are doing for the best interest of their country and the future of their children and generations to come? It reminds me of our recent general elections, where turnout was about fifteen million people out of twenty-three million people. Where were the extra eight million people? Why were voters so apathetic? Was it because of the long queues in the polling stations? Was it because our people had no citizenship identity cards? Was it because of violence and intimidation by the police and security organs? Was it because they didn't see any sense in politicians and political parties? Or was it because they were simply irresponsible citizens? How were our electoral campaigns conducted? Let's discuss together two issues of concern—first, the elements of the election cycle (as shown in the chart below), and second, the electoral campaign. In my view, these are the best two areas of concentration if we want to have all the registered voters turn out and vote on Election Day.

1. Elements of the Electoral Period in the Election Cycle

No.	Electoral period	Element of the electoral period	Specific issues	Risk of causing violence	Possibility of causing voter apathy	Strategies for improving
	Preelections	Planning	Budget and funding	When the budget is uncertain and there is not enough money for all the expenses in manning elections	If there is no clarity on the logistical arrangements and electoral staff are boycotting	Initiation of basket fund for funding of elections activities
			Staff recruitment	When the EMB have incompetent staff or staff who are competent but are not well trained on the process	When there is failure in managing the entire process at one point in time	Train more, train well, make your staff competent
			Logistics and security	When the EMB has poor logistical arrangements	When the process is interfered with	Stakeholder consultation
			Procurement	Late procurement and inadequate funding for procurement	When procurement deadlines mismatch elections calendar	Early procurement
		Training	Develop procedure	When there is no clear procedure	If voters are not aware of the procedures	Early procedural explanations of the entire process
			Operational training for electoral officials	When training materials are insufficient and TOTs are not well conducted	Electoral officials' failure to handle issues	Timely, effective, and adequate training of electoral staff

		Information	Voter and civic education	When voters are not given enough education on voting procedures	When voter education provided is not regulated	Provide enough voter and civic education while ensuring none provide it without the verification of responsible institutions
			Shareholder liaison	When laws governing relationships are violated	When there is little or low shareholder involvement	Liaise on more shareholder involvement and seek for mutual understanding and benefits
			Observer accreditation	When there are no clear accreditation procedures	When observers are not coordinated	Clear coordination processes and mechanisms are put in place
		Registration	Parties and financing	When there is no clear source of funds and no accountability on expenditures	When there is no funding to sensitize followers and agents	Reduce the number of political parties constitutionally and do more government funding
			Party registration	When there is no limitation on registration of political parties	When there are no funds for campaigning and candidates are intimidated by the incumbent government	Reduce the number of political parties constitutionally and do more government funding
			Voter registration	When there is no clear voters roll	Mixed voters roll, meaning voters find themselves in different polling stations	Clear voters roll complemented by clear voters technology
2	**During election**	**Nomination**	Party nominations	When the majority votes are ignored	That the one elected by members is dropped in favor of one selected by party leaders	Respecting the views of party members and their choices

	Campaign	Candidate nominations	If disputes are not well handled	Objections against nomination of a candidate	Handling nominations of candidates with great care
		Campaign coordination	If campaign messages violate the elections law	Interference with campaign schedules and the use of languages	Well-coordinated and regulated elections campaigns
		Media access	If media is biased	When media communicates in a way to sensitize violence	Train and regulate media on the media and elections issues
		Printing and distribution of ballot papers	If ballot papers are printed late	Clear editing of the ballot	Early editing and printing of the ballot papers
		Dispute resolutions	If there is no expertise in dispute resolution	When there is bias in resolving disputes	More training and ensuring that disputes are duly dealt with
	Voting	Special and external voting	Control of registered voters	Identifying the exact number of interested voters	Put laws in place to allow external voting, etc.
		Voting	When there is a lack of voting materials or access to voting	If the real voters don't find themselves in the voters roll	Clear and transparent voting procedures
		Technology	When there is no clear voting technology	If voters are not aware of the chosen technology	Choose simple and cheap yet proper technology for voting
	Results	Counting	Violating counting procedures	If procedures are not followed	Sensitize or train on vote-counting procedures
		Tabulations	Agree on tabulation procedure	If tabulations are ignored	Sensitize and train or agree on tabulation procedure
		Complaints and appeals	If bias is exercised	If courts and tribunals are biased	Court procedures to prevail

			Official results	When results are manipulated	When the entire process is not transparent and inclusive	Ascertain inclusivity and transparency of the official results at each stage
3	**After elections**	Review	Audit	Unclear audit report	When audit reports are cooked	Adhere to all financial regulations for accountability
			Evaluations	Cooked evaluations reports	Nonparticipatory or noninclusive evaluations	Inclusive and participatory evaluations
		Reforms	Legal reform proposals	Poor legal reforms	Reforms that are not based on on-the-ground information	Do an exhaustive information and fact finding before you do reforms
			Archiving and research	When there are no archives	When real data is not archived	Proper archiving mechanisms and means
			EMB reforms	Reforms that favor a few stakeholders	Pressurized/ biased reforms or reforms that are not based on research	Do research before you reform
		Strategy	Institutional strengthening and professional development	When institution is full of incompetent staff	Unqualified staff who coordinate elections while intimidating stakeholders	Organizational turnaround, or conduct an ID/ OS analysis before you do the strengthening
			Voter register updates	Name omission in the voters roll	When there is no solution to registered voters who are omitted from the voters roll	Clean voters roll, complemented by simple and clear voter-registration procedures
			Networking			
			Electoral systems and boundaries			

The chart above offers hints to but does not cover all the reasons why voters are apathetic. Each country, in its own setting, might have different reasons, and as these hints address commonalities, you will need to adjust them to your own situation. As we saw in Namibia, polling stations had long queues, and the number who turned out as compared to registered voters was above 80 percent.

2. *The Effect of the Electoral Campaign on Voter Turnout*

Elections, even small local ones, can be stressful, costly, and time-consuming. Therefore, if you enter one, you need to be prepared to take all measures to make it worth your while. Learning how to win a campaign will lead to great success in the end. They normally start a day after candidates are nominated and end a day before voting or the election itself. The election campaign, as seen in the election cycle above, is where many disputes appear and need to be resolved amicably to ensure free and peaceful elections. For you to be able to run a successful campaign, you need to digest (at least) the following three things:

    i. Information
   ii. Media
  iii. Preparation

Information

a) You need to prepare or gather the sort of information voters will expect to hear from you. Include your rationale, why should they choose you, what you will do for them, what makes you a better candidate, and so forth.

b) What's your story? Why do you want to be elected? Provide your biography.

c) What are your values, core convictions, principles, and passions?

d) What about the issues? Include foreign policy and economic issues, tax laws, environmental laws, immigration policy, social issues such as flooding and global warming, and your entire worldview.

e) What makes you better than your opponent? You should be able to describe and market yourself, or else voters will believe all the evils your opponent is spreading about you.

Media

Media simply the means of mass communication. For effective campaigning, the following elements must be carefully observed:

a) The candidate: You as a candidate need to be presentable, well dressed, and sober during the entire campaign period. Prepare for debates and present yourself to the press in your best condition.

b) Website: If possible, prepare a website, update it regularly, collect feedback through email, make contribution links visible on all pages, and post videos, commercials, and press releases.

c) Social media: Use Facebook, Twitter, LinkedIn, Instagram, Google Plus, TV and radio presentations, persuasion emails, and so on.

Preparation

The last thing when planning for your campaign, try to understand the following:

a) political affiliation of the electorate
b) turnout patterns
c) income and education levels of voters
d) issues such as economic levels, unemployment rates, and social values
e) preliminary budget and plan for fundraising
f) understanding of media outlets

4

You Are Now Crossing the UK Border

When traveling abroad, you will need a valid passport and visa to enter that specific country. You will also need an international vaccination card, popularly known as a yellow card. After you have departed your airport to your destination, you will be assumed to have already entered that specific country. When traveling to UK via Dubai in 2010, I wondered about the immigration clearance procedures at Heathrow International Airport. Upon my arrival, I proceeded through the queue and was asked, "What's brings you to the UK, and for how long?"

"I come on duty for seven days," I replied.

My passport was stamped, and after passing the immigration officer, I came across a signboard reading, "You are now crossing the UK border." I was amazed, as I had presumed I was already in the UK after landing. Why was I crossing the border only after passing the final immigration checkpoint? I had a chat with several people and was told that at Heathrow International Airport, you cannot be granted entry if do not satisfy the immigration department, even if you have an entry visa.

A number of questions arose in my head about this concept. If I satisfied the UK embassy in my home country and I had a return ticket, why would I need to explain myself at the airport? I thought my visa needed to be confirmed as legitimate and stamped and that was it. But here, it is not the case. In my opinion, this is harassment and embarrassing to visitors who go to the UK. I would ask the UK Border Agency to change this and be respectful to other nationalities, especially those of the African continent. I don't recall ever having seen such irritating and embarrassing signage at our points of entry, be it the Julius Nyerere International Airport, Kilimanjaro International Airport, or our lake and sea ports.

However, at Dubai Airport, even though there were very big crowds of people, and despite the lack of limitations and insinuating signboards and statements, it was safe and secure. Travelling abroad from Africa should not be seen as running away from problems and seeking safe haven in Europe or America. In one of my trips to Europe, travelling on Kenya Airways to Amsterdam, I recall being asked by the immigration officer just as I got out of the plane, "What brings you to Holland?"

"Training," I replied.

"Where?"

"Ede," I replied.

"Which college or school?"

"The MDF."

I was given my passport back. My Kenyan colleague, on being asked what brought him to Holland, simply replied, "Spending." I am sure that at the embassy in Dar Es Salaam, if you say you are traveling as a tourist, the consulars would want you to disclose your bank account details. Does this apply to them when requesting visas to come to our countries? This is a nuisance, and it must be stopped. I am happy where I am. I am happy at home, and if I am requesting a visa to any country, they should know that I have plans for it and I mean it.

Looking at it from another perspective, this could be seen as a protection of UK civilians' rights. This reminds me of citizenship. Am I a responsible citizen to my country? Would I be able to defend what was meant for my people even if it meant embarrassing people from other nationalities? The answer should be yes. When President Magufuli called for a review of all mining contracts, he did embarrass Acacia Mining Ltd and its entire business process, but yes, he did it for the best interest of our country. Was it properly handled? Did that process have a negative impact on our economy? How about our international relations? And what relief did we get from those negotiations? Were all these negotiations carried out in relation to our mining policy? Do you think there is a need for public policy review in all sectors that contribute a major share of our GDP? Let's look closely at the following statistics. You will realize by yourself how some government decisions can negatively affect the economy.

Tanzania has achieved high growth rates based on its vast natural resource wealth and tourism with GDP growth in 2009-17 averaging 6%-7% per year. Dar Es Salaam used fiscal stimulus measures and easier monetary policies to lessen the impact of the global recession and in general, benefited from low oil prices. Tanzania has largely completed its transition to a market economy, though the government retains a presence in sectors such as telecommunications, banking, energy, and mining.

The economy depends on agriculture, which accounts for slightly less than one-quarter of GDP and employs about 65% of the work force, although gold production in recent years has increased to about 35% of exports. All land in Tanzania is owned by the government, which can lease land for up to 99 years. Proposed reforms to allow for land ownership, particularly foreign land ownership, remain unpopular.

The financial sector in Tanzania has expanded in recent years and foreign-owned banks account for about 48% of the banking industry's total assets.

Competition among foreign commercial banks has resulted in significant improvements in the efficiency and quality of financial services, though interest rates are still relatively high, reflecting high fraud risk. Banking reforms have helped increase private-sector growth and investment.

The World Bank, the IMF, and bilateral donors have provided funds to rehabilitate Tanzania's aging infrastructure, including rail and port, which provide important trade links for inland countries. In 2013, Tanzania completed the world's largest Millennium Challenge Compact (MCC) grant, worth $698 million, but in late 2015, the MCC Board of Directors deferred a decision to renew Tanzania's eligibility because of irregularities in voting in Zanzibar and concerns over the governments use of a controversial cybercrime bill."

Under the new government elected in 2015, Tanzania has developed an ambitious development agenda focused on creating a better business environment through improved infrastructure, access to financing, and education progress, but implementing budgets remains challenging for the government. Recent policy moves by President MAGUFULI are aimed at protecting domestic industry and have caused concern among foreign investors.[1]

So if the MCC board deferred a decision to renew our country's eligibility because of irregularities in voting in Zanzibar and concerns over government use of a controversial cybercrime bill, what would the effect be as the consortium of foreign investors in Tanzania reacted to the awkward decision we might have made?

---

[1] World Factbook.

5

Namaste, Taj Mahal

The Taj Mahal is a UNESCO World Heritage site found in the town of Agra, some 289 kilometers south of India's capital, New Delhi, and about 280 kilometers from the modern new city of Noida. The highway to Agra has three lanes to and three lanes from, installed with a toll barrier in between, and I experienced some delay after our driver was supposed to pay the fine and was lamenting. This highway is digitized, so anything happening on the road can be seen from a control room. Taj simply means "crowns," while Mahal means "a place."

It is an enormous mausoleum complex commissioned in 1632 by the Mughal emperor Shah Jahan to house the remains of his beloved wife who bored 11 children after the first wife could not give a child to the King. Constructed over a 20-year period on the southern bank of the Yamuna River in Agra, India, the famed complex is one of the most outstanding examples of Mughal architecture, which combined Indian, Persian and Islamic influences. At its center is the Taj Mahal itself, built of shimmering white marbles gathered from Zimbabwe that seems to change color depending on the daylight. Designated a UNESCO World Heritage site in 1983, it remains one of the world's most celebrated structures and a stunning symbol of India's rich history.

The story above was displayed at a prestigious theater close to the Taj Mahal. The theater was constructed over a period of fifteen years, and it is considered to be one of the classiest theaters in the world. At the Taj Mahal itself, me and my fellow electoral officers received a formal presentation from the professional tour guide at the site. If the United Republic of Tanzania could only see how many buses were carrying tourists to and from Agra, she would reform its national parks and game reserves to ensure accessibility and accommodation. From fancy technology shows to eminent buildings and sports infrastructure to machinery farming on roadside farms, we Tanzanians need to change our mind-set to ensure sustainable development and remarkable progress for future generations.

India's rich tourism sites and parks have been developed from a combination of ancient Indian culture and technology around Delhi. If Tanzania's tourism is to be competitive, it must likewise be redeveloped using a combination of our ancient history, culture, natural wealth, reserves, and technology. If you go to Bujora in June or July, you will see many amazing sights, but the documentation and development (in terms of buildings and other structures) is extremely poor. If we could embark on redeveloping our tourism, including sites such as the Butiama Mwl Nyerere Mausoleum, the Bujora Cultural Museum, Maswa, Bagamoyo, Kwihala, Ujiji, the Buha Kingdom of Herujuu, Mwanamalundi of Shinyanga, Isike, and Milambo history, in terms of art and poetry, surely our tourism sector would see amazing improvement.

At Delhi International Airport, we were welcomed along with the Indian diplomats and cleared immediately by immigration. This signifies the rich kindness of Asians. The Delhi Aero City, which was being developed, demonstrated how serious the leadership and people are in some countries. I would urge our ministers and permanent secretaries to work as hard as they can to make sure our country is left with a legacy of trustworthy leadership. Honorable Kessy, an MP for the Nkasi constituency, was seen lamenting in the Parliament on May 8, 2018, that all leaders and everyone with authority should join President Magufuli's effort in building the economy and providing better social services. On the same date, the MP for Monduli, the Honorable James Kalanga, was seen lamenting that the minister for water had lied to the Parliament when presenting his 2018/19 annual budget, when he said that the previous budget was implemented at a 56 percent rate while other sources and government documents revealed a 26 percent budget implementation. Now, if a minister can lie to a supreme government arm like the Parliament, where do you think our country is heading? Yes, we plan very well and do budgeting, but why do we implement our annual budget at such a low rate? I would urge that we develop a sense of monitoring and evaluation on the performance of ministers and other executive or principal government leaders publicly, and if we find that, out of negligence and failure to deliver, one has not attained 75 percent, we should remove that official immediately; we need to hold all those with authority accountable to their responsibility.

Meanwhile, we need to the failure and success of our investments. Consider the elegant, fast UDART buses. Where are they stocked? Jangwani, right? What happened? Twenty-nine buses were found mechanically damaged as a result of flooding. Were the project managers not aware of what Jangwani looks like during rain seasons? How many billions of shillings were wasted simply because of this negligent incompetence in making decisions or in advising the government? Can we imitate India's investors? How many hotels do we have at Julius Nyerere International Airport? Or Kilimanjaro International Airport? Can our visitors experience the comfort we would expect while in other countries? Let us rethink and renovate. Our airports are sorely detached from normal life; there is no cheap public transport at the airports, such as railway or commuter buses, only private taxi services. Where are the hotels? Is it an issue of security or a failure to plan for elegant structures? Is it because of the unclear business-licensing procedures? Or is it due to the bribes one must pay when looking for a business license? Do you think if we automated licensing, businesses in all categories would flourish and hence increase government revenue? How do we control business registration and business licensing? How about air business licensing? Why are prices so high?

Flying from Dar es Salaam to Delhi, for example, is always possible via several routes, depending on the carrier. I traveled to Delhi via Muscat using Oman Air. En route, I familiarized myself with the aviation magazine and became interested by the story of the Oman Air chief executive officer who turned the company around. According to the story, the CEO was hired when the company had very few flights, but after some time passed, he managed to increase the number of flights as well as the number of international routes Do you think this result came out of nowhere? It's clear that the Oman people had a vision for where they wanted to go after a certain period of time; they told the CEO what they expected from his work and where Oman Air was supposed to go. I believe that if Tanzania had enchanted their way to go with ATCL, we would soon be seeing fares cut down as a number of flights increased. This act would create more demand and hence sustain our air transport systems. There are vivid examples of this business practice within and outside Africa, so it is possible. Have you ever considered what Rwandair did to have such a good number of flights only twenty-four years after the Rwandan genocide, where all government and economic systems were blocked and/or interfered with? What made them revamp their economy, developing after only twenty-four years an airline that can take you into the world? And it is a competitive airline, with fancy airplanes that use the latest technologies, and, moreover, is the cheapest within the East African community. As I am writing this page today, on October 13, 2018, it comes into my mind that tomorrow will be the commemoration of the late Mwl.

Julius Kambarage Nyerere, the first president of Tanzania and the father of our nation, who used to say, "It can be done. Just play your part."

Can we stick to our Wings of Kilimanjaro? I believe that if we have the right people with the capacity to manage it transparently and strategically, our country will add another major contributor to our national income and gross domestic product as well. Can ATCL learn a greater story than the ones taught by Oman Air and Rwandair? Let's learn from their path but follow our dream.

If ATCL is to capture Tanzania's local aviation market, I can see them buying brand-new tourist Land Cruisers to transport tourists from Chato Airport to Biharamulo, Burigi, and Rwakimisi Game Reserves, driving tourists to Moyowosi Game Reserve from Kigoma Airport. I can see ATCL buying speedboats to transfer tourists to Gombe National Park (the home of mountain gorillas) and small planes or helicopters to take tourists to Mahale (another home of mountain gorillas), and Katavi National Park (the home of white giraffes), if not Serengeti National Park and Ngorongoro and Embakai Craters. Ngorongoro Crater is home to the Big Five and is home to thirty-three thousand different animals. Embakai Crater remains a popular breeding site for flamingos worldwide. I can see ATCL boats ferrying tourists around Saanane Game Reserve and the Ukerewe Dancing Stones. In general, ATCL. has to have an entire transport supply chain business to reap what is expected from our Bombardiers and other fleets that will be purchased by the company.

I can see a fleet-management portfolio increasing from aviation to land and water vessel management. Our Bombardiers will count more if the tourism sector is revamped for the better. All the game reserves, national parks, and conservation areas, be they water or land or space, might be more accessible, and the walk-in and walk-through should be guaranteed—if I have paid to see a lion, I must see a lion. It should not be left up to chance. We must have guides who know exactly where the lions are located.

Dumela Gaborone

I traveled to Gaborone, Botswana, for the first time in 2012. I stayed at the Gaborone Sun Hotel. In 2015, I went for the second time and stayed at Phakalane Golf Estate. On both these occasions, I was very much amazed by the elephant statue constructed from ivory. *Is it real ivory?* I asked myself. It amazed me how many elephants might have been killed to collect such a large amount of ivory. How much ivory went undiscovered after the elephants were killed? So many questions arose. I considered that there must be an abundance of wildlife. The size and level of advancement of the tourism business in Botswana left me wide-mouthed with wonder whenever I was in the suburbs of Gaborone.

On finding more about Botswana tourism, I came to learn that tourism in Botswana includes walking through special areas, bird-watching, hiking, fishing, adventures, arts and crafts, community, culture and history, leisure and lifestyle, natural attractions, routes and trails, trans-frontiers, and wildlife safaris. I was amazed by how the leisure and lifestyle mode of tourism was cherished by local people of Botswana. Other leisure and lifestyle tourist attractions include the Phakalane Gold Estate, developed by former vice president of Botswana, David. N. Magang.

With the developments in rail transport after the completion of the standard gauge railway in Tanzania, the private sector as a whole and individual businessmen have something to learn. They will have to build hotels and lodges nearly everywhere where there is a game reserve or a national park, hence reducing lodging costs. The costs are too high, to the extent that lodging in game reserves and national parks is an expensive luxury, not an option for normal citizens. Food in hotels and lodgings should also be as cheap as eating a home-cooked meal. This will promote tourism and business development. If you want to eat octopus at the Forodhani Market in Zanzibar, it is extremely expensive, and yet if you go to the suburbs of Chakechake, in Pemba, octopus is as cheap as eating a meal at home. My argument is that we should develop the food and beverage sector to the extent that eating or cooking at home will be seen as unnecessary, and that's when domestic tourism will flourish.

I has wondered, how could our country benefit from the huge urban populations of our country? How can we modernize our leisure and lifestyle industry while maintaining affordable prices in all of our beach hotels—in Dar Es Salaam and Zanzibar, the Lake Victoria beaches and Lake Tanganyika valley beach hotels, or even in the Lake Rukwa beaches? Most of our beaches are still virgin, and on those beaches where there are few hotels, the prices are overwhelming to the extent that most of them rely on foreign tourists to generate revenue.

How can the United Republic of Tanzania maximize revenue collection from all our tourist attractions, ranging from donkey riding on the Nairobi ranges to Embakai flamingo breeding sites all the way to Oldonyo Lengai mountain climbing down to Lake Natron flamingo breeding sites? How can we maximize the Pinyinyi-Engaresero Hot Springs and the Engaresero Footprints and Waterfalls? I challenge the authorities in Tanzania to modernize and document the Sale culture and traditional *boma*s and all Maasai cultural *boma*s around the Ngorongoro District Council. In all the game reserves across the country, in the national parks, and even in our bushes and the Miombo Woodland in West Tanzania and elsewhere, there should be a public means of transport to make them accessible to local people. Then, slowly, the culture of partying and taking holidays locally will be cultivated in our children and in generations to come.

In almost all of the thirty-one regions of Tanzania, there is a tourist attraction—a cultural or historical site, a game reserve, a national park, a waterfall, or a savanna. Try to imagine how the slave route from the Ujiji Slave Market to the Tabora Kwihala Museum could benefit if it were developed to suit modern history, culture, and education? What if the Bagamoyo Slave Market and the Kwere and Arab cultural *bomas* and traditions were properly documented to suit modern tourism? How about Chief Melele of the Safwa and the war he fought—what if it could be documented and digitally displayed in the SAFWA Museum of Utengule (if there was one)? How about displays in the Chief Milambo Museum of *ruga-ruga* soldiers? But if you go to Tabora, there is nothing to show you that there were once very strong chiefdoms of the Unyanyembe, who introduced taxation for the first time in the history of Tanganyika traders and chiefdoms. Is this because of negligence? Or is it due to a lack of exposure and experience of those charged with responsibilities to oversee our cultural development? What budget has the Parliament passed for tourism and cultural sector development? Where exactly do we want to go in terms of tourism and culture?

7

The Legacy of the Poor

As a closing chapter, I thought it might be wise to share what ought to be accomplished by the leaders of postcolonial and independent Africa. The continent has been characterized by poor educational systems and very poor health systems, resulting in malnutrition. Most African countries have undergone serious transformations in their leadership, governance, and economy, and they survived the winds of betrayal, neocolonialism, and lack of exposure in many aspects of development, ranging from clear development policies to governance and political policies, which caused our countries to deteriorate not only in terms of huge expenditures and borrowing from foreign countries but also embezzlement and fraud and poor public-policy management.

However, a number of leaders have emerged who might be termed as "true sons of Africa" because of their vision and their contribution to the development of their respective countries, and to the Black Continent at large. Have you ever heard of Mwl Julius Kambarage Nyerere of the United Republic of Tanzania? How about Nkwame Nkrumah of Ghana? Or even Patrice Emely Lumumba of the Congo and Nelson Mandela of South Africa? Robert Gabriel Mugabe of Zimbabwe and Keneth Kaunda of Zambia? Or even Thomas Sankara of the Upper Volta, just to mention a few?

What legacy did all the leaders I mentioned leave for the countries and for the entire continent of Africa? Can those leaders strive to leave their countries a legacy to match their dreams? Africa is not poor at all, but its people are. There are many resources in Africa, which, if well utilized, will transform this continent to be the best one of all. It's not the hidden truth that all these leaders went through missionary schools. Had they been denied education, their history would not be the same as it is today.

Who is to be blamed for today's Congo, for example? Is it still the Belgians? Or is it the Americans? In my view, the answer is neither. The Congolese have themselves to blame; all the bloodshed and the country's civil unrest lies in the hands of the Congolese people, their government, their religious leaders, Congolese tribe chiefs, and traditional leaders. Also, the Congolese educational system is to be blamed. It is not acceptable to blame everything on the Americans and Belgians. Try to imagine a country having more than two hundred political parties. Seriously? All these want to be presidents and ministers of the DRC? It's chaos! Is there any vision of Congolese politics in the constitution of the DRC? There is a lot of work to be done in overhauling the Congolese constitution. Who shot Kabila? Belgians or Americans? Definitely not! The Congolese killed Kabila, and in many such ways, we Africans are responsible for our own problems and our own underdevelopment.

How about Thomas Sankara?

> He was Burkina Faso's president from August 1983 until his assassination on October 15, 1987. Perhaps, more than any other African president in living memory, Thomas Sankara, in four years, transformed Burkina Faso from a poor country, dependent on aid, to an economically independent and socially progressive nation.[2]

---

[2] Wikipedia.

If he managed to transform his nation from a poor one to an economically independent and socially progressive one, why kill him? Who killed him, Western forces or Africans rebellions? How many African countries are economically independent and socially progressive today by their own sweat? Can President Magufuli beat this record? Are we supporting him? Is he a true son of Africa? In my opinion, he is going to beat this record if he is assisted by all Tanzanians. I tell you, if we fail to overhaul our economic dependence and social programs during the Magufuli era, it will take decades further to find a leader of the same caliber. This is not to mention what has been accomplished by statesmen such as Mwl Julius Kambarage Nyerere. How are our institutions looking? Are they bureaucratic and corrupt? What does the corruption report say about our institutions? Are they capable of delivering the services they were meant to provide? What does building sixty-seven district hospitals in one year mean to you? Is our president overhauling the provision of health services in the country? How about free education? Consider the recent stingy message of the president, in May 2018, that he will not increase salaries apart from the statutory increments. Let's get our act together and help this man build this country.

Can we achieve excellence on our own? Where did Sankara get these vaccines for the Burkinabe children? Why could he achieve this excellence while, in other countries, things were deteriorating. Yet even today, issues of bureaucracy, corruption, irresponsibility, and lack of accountability plague the nations. How do we spend our foreign-aid packages? Are they well spent and well managed? How do we ensure the level of accomplishment in all these projects reaches excellence, to the satisfaction of the donor community? And for how long are we going be a donor-dependent country? What are we supposed to do to be a donor-free country? I am pleading with every one of you, my fellow citizens and those who are reading this book, to be of good use to your respective countries. There have been a number of poverty-alleviation programs over many years. What have their impact been? Are we still dependent on foreign aid so we do not deforest our land? Are we still dependent on foreign-funded programs to start planting trees? Let us be serious and demonstrate that we can do anything, *anything*, without foreign aid.

Where did our ginneries go? Who distorted them? What has happened in our cotton farms? Why did we quit massive cotton farming? Why did the Tabora Textiles fail to operate, ceasing their operations? Why did Mwanza, Mbeya, Musoma, Sungura, and Rafiki textiles fail? What is the overhaul plan? Do we all wait until the president decides on them? Is it necessary to depend on foreign markets to buy our cotton while we, in turn, buy clothing from India and Europe and China or even Turkey? Let's get our act together and transform farming and agricultural products processing.

Are you aware of how our forests are being abused by improper farming techniques in Tabora, Kigoma, Katavi, and Geita? Can we intervene on proper tobacco-farming techniques? What will be the result if we let our brothers from Sukumaland continue to keep thousands of cattle, deforesting wherever they are? What is the immediate solution? Do we leave it for the president to decide for us as well? How long shall this continue? Please, let us prioritize and plan to mitigate these calamities. Our country is as beautiful as heaven. We have everything we need here. Let us maintain and upgrade our various sectors and make sure the generations to come inherit a beautiful home.

But when we act on the ambition to transform our institutions and societies, we might be doing certain things wrong, ignoring the existence of other important organs. How can a president run all alone in the streets? Does he understand what it means to be a head of state, who has transformed a society in only four years? Magufuli, don't do the same. Leave other special institutions to do their professional work and be responsible for their own faults. Do the proper work, but never ignore the importance of your helpers and advisers. Do it perfectly, and by the time you are leaving in 2020, you will have left us a legacy to remember, a legacy of you,

Mr. President, for you are leading your fellow poor Tanzanians. I believe that Thomas Sankara ignored the existence of the protocol, and that's why he was seen running alone in the suburbs of Ouagadougou. My argument is that despite our driving forces to engineer positive changes in economics, politics, and development, in general, let's make it with our people, the people attached to our daily lives, the people responsible for our own security, the people responsible for our own well-being. Doctors should be allowed to act as doctors, engineers as engineers, soldiering men and women as soldiers, and nurses as nurses. Everyone in the implementation circle must be respected and supported to do his or her work, responsibly. And whenever there is incompetence, we must not hesitate to act accordingly.

> The present generation of Africans is thirsty, searching for where to draw the moral, intellectual and spiritual courage to effect change. The waters to quench the thirst, as other continents have already established, lies fundamentally in history - in Africa's forbears, men, women and children who experienced much of what most Africans currently experience, but who chose to toe a different path. The media, entertainment industry, civil society groups, writers, institutions and organizations must begin to search out and include African role models, case studies and examples in their contents. For Africans, the strength desperately needed for the transformation of the continent cannot be drawn from World Bank and IMF policies, from aid and assistance obtained from China, India, the United States or Europe. The strength to transform Africa lies in the foundations laid by uncommon heroes like Thomas Sankara; a man who showed Africa and the world that with a single minded pursuit

of purpose, the worst can be made the best, and in
record time too.[3]

Go, Magufuli, go. Go running, go walking, and go flying. Go,
Mr. President, go. If they ask you why you are running, tell them,
"I am running for my people." Go, Magufuli, go! Whether you like
it or not, Mr. President, you have enemies. You have enemies both
from within your country and from outside the country. You also
have enemies from within your political party, CCM. All those who
are seemingly not in favor of your policies and leadership style are
your enemies. You eat with them, you sleep with them, you travel
with them, and yet they are your enemies. My advice to you, Mr.
Magufuli, is "Don't give up!" Your cause is eternal, and every one
of us, the Wananchi (countrymen), should support you, from left
and right and from up and down. May you run faster than the wind
and rain, escaping all traps and setups. However, Mr. President
you ought to be responsible for whatever you are doing—not only
responsible but also friendly and transparent, to the extent that we,
the Wananchi, will have no reservations about telling your tale.
For example, the recent missing one and a half trillion should be
declared amicably and by responsible institutions and not fake or
unauthorized spokespersons.

Mr. President, the legacy you are building will leave our country
in such a state that when people from other places come to visit,
your name will be praised and you will be called a very poor man.
Poor not in terms of wealth and material possession but in terms
of a humbled heart, which could not pump blood properly until it
saw a better living for your people. But this legacy, Mr. President,
won't be attained if your deputy president, prime minister, ministers,
permanent secretaries, directors, the Parliament, and the judiciary
do not change their mind-set and echo your dreams and visions. I
am saying this because of the behavior we have demonstrated in key

---

[3] Wikipedia.

revenue collections points. If we do not change our mind-set to have that sense of responsibility and fulfillment of all our commissioned tasks, nothing will change for the better. Follow me in the examples I am going to highlight below.

I. Rovos Train

This is a five-star private luxury train that travels a distance of more than six thousand kilometers, from Cape Town, in South Africa, to the Indian Ocean coasts of Dar es Salaam. While in South Africa, it starts in Cape Town, then stops at Kimberley for the tourists to enjoy town life and the breathtaking beauty of the diamond museum. In Pretoria, they enjoy the smoke show from old steam engines. Can you ask yourself, what did we do with our old train engines? Did we sell them to India? Is any one of you thinking of having a railway museum in Dar es Salaam where all the railway development phases may be showcased? How about the strategy of using train stops as a source of income for all the game reserves across Tanzania? The rivers and ponds? Hills and ranges and valleys and the savannah? Are any of our railway directors thinking outside the box? Do we have enough carriages to accommodate private travel? Have you ever imagined why the Saba Trade Exhibition's private train to Selous is fully booked in such a short time? Why wouldn't TANAPA and TAZARA forge synergies to increase government revenue and their annual collections? Why is there no tour program for the Rovos train's stops at Makambako in Tanzania? How far is the Usangu Game Reserve from Makambako? How about Kitulo National Park and the famous Ruaha National Park? We are not serious about capitalizing on our opportunities. The tour program for this train can bring in thousands of dollars, let alone our new Standard gauge railway, currently under construction, if well managed and planned. How do we sell train tickets? Certainly I am crying over this, as all the efforts of our country will be wasted if we will fail to manage the SGR train and make the maximum use of private trains to

Simanjiro, Tarangire, Arusha, Moshi, and Korogwe, to see what our country has to offer in terms of tourist-attraction sites, culture, and traditions.

II. Trans-Siberian Train

This is a private luxury train that travels a distance of more than eight thousand kilometers, from Moscow, in Russia, through Mongolia to Beijing, South China. In Russia, the Trans-Siberian train stops in more than five railway stations, and in each station, travelers get a chance to look at various tourist attractions, including national parks and rivers, like Angara River and Lake Baikal. In Mongolia, the train stops more than three times. In each area where it stops, travelers get a chance to look at various tourist attractions, as they do in Russia. These stops help raise the income for the mentioned countries, as tourists spend a lot during their safari.

Tanzania, as one of the countries reforming its transportation system, has a lesson to learn on how aviation, railway, and road transport business is done. Railway business in Tanzania has to be transformed so it can accommodate private trains for the highest and middle earners to enjoy the breathtaking beauty of our country's savannahs, parks, rivers, lakes, and terrains. We have almost everything in terms of natural resources and natural parks and sites. If we can develop them and modernize our stations and restaurants, like the Nyama Choma at Saranda Railways station and Mnadani in Dodoma, our visitors will have memorable and breathtaking journeys. If the appropriate advice is taken into account, surely, our tourism sector will boom, raising internal revenues.

III. Desert Express Namibia

The Desert Express is an exclusive chartered train that travels from Windhoek Railway Station, going south of Namibia and then west to the coast of the Atlantic Ocean and finally north to Namibia's largest national park (Etosha National Park), with its variety of big game. This private train has been designed to take tourists on safari in various tourist sites, such as the Quiver Tree Forest, where some trees are believed to be more than three hundred years old, various fascinating and spectacular landscapes ranging from dams to dunes, and the Kalahari Desert. No wonder Tanzania has done its best to draw high amounts of foreign money to its national reserves. Can you imagine a park with only Oryx antelopes and squirrels attracting tourists at such a level? How would a Tarangire National Park do? How about the Simanjiro Game Reserve and the Loliondo game-controlled areas? I agree—the Namib Shifting Sand Dunes are larger than our shifting sands near Olduvai Gorge, but how about the Embakai flamingo viewing and that at Engaresero, near Lake Natron, where a splendid view of the flamingos' colors at their breeding sites creates such breathtaking beauty? Imagine having gourmet breakfast, lunch, and dinner at the exotic Namibian landscapes. This should be a value-added feature of the railway business, but try traveling on our railway and see how badly a customer can be treated onboard. You can't even get a glass of wine despite our Dodoma winery industries; we don't praise our own products. Instead, we get lunches and dinners containing rice and maize mash, as if someone is receiving medical treatment, where you have to take the same bland meal two or three times a day.

All in all, I would like to commend the overhauling of our infrastructure and transportation system. Recently, I lost my cousin-brother, and I needed to figure out how I was going to transport the dead body from Dar es Salaam to Kigoma. The buses wanted a total of Tsh 2,800,000 to 2,500,000. However, surprisingly, on inquiring with ATCL, it cost us 930,000 from Dar to Kigoma. This was a relief, and I would plead with you, Mr. President, to make sure by the time you reach the end of your term you are leaving this country with a full-fledged transport system to help your people choose a transport of their choice, depending on their budget and preference. The *Irish Observer* has reported a boom of tourists from Ireland to

Tanzania, an increase of more than 300 percent. Can we continue this trend? Can we maintain or even improve our tourism standards to multiply these tours in the coming years? This is why I believe that our Bombardier counts and that we, all Tanzanians, should, in one way or another, support our leader, the president of the United Republic of Tanzania.

Last but not least, the recent Tanzania Federation for Football negotiated with the ATCL. to release their Boeing 787-8 Dreamliner to transport our national football team to Praia. When I first heard this from the minister for sports, I said, "Wow, what a move, and what a breakthrough." What an advantage for our national team and its supporters to travel in one vessel, where the laughter and camaraderie may lead to better performance. The government's decision to release the flight was the best move because traveling to Praia on a public transport would lead to delay and definitely defeat. However, my main problem is price options. Can you guess them? It's currently $2,000 for a business-class ticket and $1,500 for an economy ticket. Really? Are the coordinators insane? What Tanzanian is going to spend $2,000 for three days of pleasure? Do we really expect normal citizens to pay $2,000 to fly to Praia and then expect them to go make noise on the pitch? I would imagine the ATCL would make the ticket cheaper or at least subsidize them to give normal citizens the ability to go and cherish our national team. Imagine—what ATCL CSR program would help in this? Are there any possibilities for the government and TFF to intervene and subsidize these tickets so that supporters can pay less? Paying $2,000 or $1,500 might be feasible for people traveling on a long-planned vacation, but not for an abrupt trip like this one. Had the tickets been advertised three months in advance, I believe many of us could have saved up. Change your mind-set and get the right people to advise in business development. I believe ATCL management has got it all wrong by charging more for tickets to Praia. Do we have a directorate of tourism promotion and development within ATCL? If not, create one as soon as possible. How about the director of fundraising? Perhaps different ticketing strategies must be developed to accommodate different marketing strategies and segments.

About the Author

Deogratius Nsanzugwanko is an internationally semiaccredited facilitator (building resources in democracy, governance, and elections in the Middle East and Southern Africa); government employee, farmer, dream analyst (International Association for the Study of Dreams invited him for the first time in the World Dreaming History conference); and entrepreneur. He runs Kana Hatchery, an SME dedicated to improving the availability of chicken in all forms across the country. He holds a joint international MBA from the Maastricht School of Management and the Eastern and Southern Africa Management Institute. He is also a graduate of Tumaini University College (2006), where he received a postgraduate diploma in management. He has also received an advanced diploma in information technology from the Institute of Accountancy, Arusha.

He spent his first year after graduation in 2004 working for the Brothers of Charity Kigoma before he joined the National Electoral Commission in 2006, where he worked for ten years. Apart from professional life, the author has been trying his level best to give back to society, spending most of his free time working for the Rotary Club of Bahari Dar es Salaam and attaining an award as a Paul Harris Fellow.

About the Book

Airport Mysteries: The Four Business-Class Rats and Why the Wings of Kilimanjaro Counts highlights the recent accomplishments at the Julius Nyerere International Airport, terminal 2, and the newly constructed terminal 3. It also highlights development measures taken by the government in development and accountability concerning major economic issues, governance, and politics, while advising on how our government can maximize our economic potential compared to other African countries (and non-African countries the author was privileged to travel to). In the book, you will also read about tourism, culture, and religion. In the end, it is hoped that you will conclude by yourself why ATCL counts!

Printed in the United States
By Bookmasters